Freshwater

Aquariums

Manual

Freshwater Aquariums Manual

Alkeith O Jackson

Freshwater Aquariums Manual

A Beginners Guide

To Keeping And Feeding Freshwater Aquarium Fish

Alkeith O Jackson

Freshwater Aquariums Manual

Copyright Notice

Copyright © 2014 Alkeith O Jackson. All Rights Reserved.

All rights reserved. No part of this publication may be reproduced, distributed, or transmitted in any form or by any means, including photocopying, recording, or other electronic or mechanical methods, without the prior written permission of the publisher, except in the case of brief quotations embodied in critical reviews and certain other non-commercial uses permitted by copyright law.

Disclaimer and Terms of Use

This book is a general educational health-related information product. As an express condition to reading this book, you understand and agree to the following terms. The books content is not a substitute for direct, personal, professional medical care and diagnosis.

The Author and/ or Publisher of this book is not responsible in any manner whatsoever for any consequential damages that result from the use of, or the inability to use this book.

First Printing, 2014

ISBN-13: 978-1502428769

Contents

Preface: Before you Purchase an Aquarium 8
Introduction 13
Adding Plants and Animals to the Aquarium 13
Chapter 1 22
Collecting The Specimens 22
Chapter 2 25
The Best Season For 25
Collecting Water Animals 25
Chapter 3 28
Water Animals Care And Feeding 28
Chapter 4 31
Setting Up the Aquarium to Be Emptied and Filled Automatically 31
Chapter 5 35
Freshwater Snails 35
Chapter 6 37
Cleaning The Aquarium 37

Freshwater Aquariums Manual

Alkeith O Jackson

Preface: Before you Purchase an Aquarium

A Well kept and well-stocked aquarium is a very attractive object. Even a small globe with a goldfish or two is an addition to a room, and having a goldfish is far better than no pets at all.

An aquarium affords an opportunity for keeping a number of very interesting pets without any muss and with very little trouble; and even the tiny inhabitants of an aquarium will learn to recognize the person who cares for them.

Before you purchase an aquarium you should decide how large and how complete you want to have it. It is very disappointing to find your aquarium far too small to hold all the interesting creatures that you want to keep. An aquarium should never be overcrowded; it is better to have a large aquarium with few, than a small aquarium with too many, forms of animal life.

If you just want to keep goldfish or other fish, turtles, tadpoles, or newts, you can use a bowl or even a glass jar, and if the water is kept clean and the creatures are properly fed they will live and thrive for a long time.

Such an affair is not really an aquarium, however, if you want a really attractive and beautiful aquarium it must contain a number of different forms of animal life and must have enough vegetable life to balance the animals and keep the water fresh and pure.

If an aquarium is properly made and the right proportions of plants and animals are kept in it, the water will remain clear and will not require replenishing, except to replace that portion lost by evaporation.

The best form for an aquarium is rectangular and deeper than wide, and the all-glass aquariums are far better than those composed of a frame of iron or metal bottom and uprights and panes of glass.

Aquariums may be constructed at home from wood or metal and glass, but these are never satisfactory, and any person who can afford to own pets or keep an aquarium can afford to purchase one ready-made.

They are far from expensive, and a small, ready-made aquarium is far better than a large, home-made one.

If you have a pond or fountain in the yard you may convert this into an outdoor aquarium, but it will not be as interesting as the glass indoor aquarium, for you can only observe a very small portion of the water life.

Rectangular Aquarium

Freshwater Aquariums Manual

Alkeith O Jackson

Introduction

Adding Plants and Animals to the Aquarium

There are a certain number of species of aquatic animals which will live peaceably together in an aquarium, but many other species are much more aggressive and shouldn't be allowed in the same aquarium with more peaceable creatures.

Goldfish, carp, small fish of any sort, very small turtles, medium-sized water insects, and tadpoles will all get on together, and fresh-water snails of various kinds should be added. Newts or salamanders are also very interesting additions and agree well with most other inhabitants.

Avoid frogs unless they are very small; even a medium-sized frog will devour other creatures of large size. Large turtles should also be kept in a separate aquarium, and carnivorous fishes, such as pickerel, pike, and eels, should not be kept with other forms of life.

Many of our native fish are very handsome and interesting. The pretty sticklebacks build neat nests of aquatic grass and weeds within which they rest and rear their young, while the beautiful sunfish known also as roach and pumpkinseeds build nests of pebbles on the bottom of ponds and lakes.

Your aquarium should always have the bottom covered with an inch or so of washed bird gravel, for many aquatic creatures require sand, while others burrow in it.

The various kinds of dace are very attractive fish, but for all-around beauty and satisfaction you cannot find anything better than goldfish.

The ordinary, old-fashioned red or silver varieties are pretty and graceful, but some of the fancy breeds are more interesting and attractive. Some of these have long, trailing, veil-like tails; others have double or treble tails; others have elongated fins; while still others have great, goggle eyes and curious, stub noses.

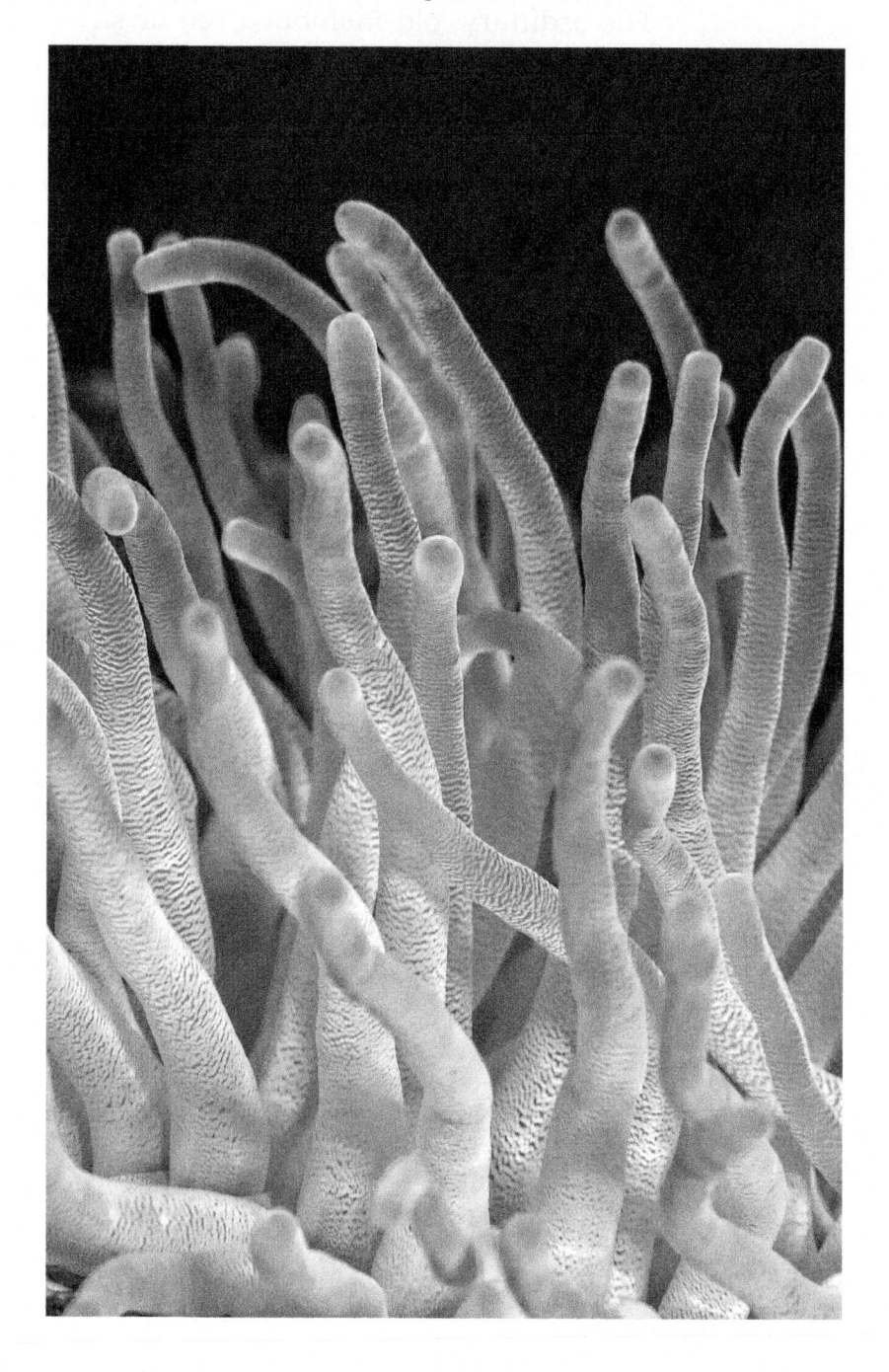

Freshwater Aquariums Manual

In Japan goldfish have been bred for odd forms and striking peculiarities for centuries and there are over one hundred named varieties known.

A few tadpoles are always interesting, and whether these are the young of frogs or of salamanders you can watch them develop into adults and find a great deal of interest while doing so. If the tadpoles are those of frogs the hind legs will sprout first, whereas if they are the young of salamanders the front feet will first appear.

Many water insects are suitable for the aquarium and the funny water boatmen that skim about on the surface of pools and ponds should find a place in every home aquarium.

The shining, black water-beetles are also good, and it is great fun to watch these fellows dive to the bottom of the water with their air supply in the form of glistening, silvery bubbles. The odd caddice-fly larvae are also droll and interesting creatures.

These are caterpillar-like larvae that make odd little homes of tiny pebbles, sticks, or shells and live on the bottoms of brooks and ponds. They retreat within their little houses when disturbed, and crawl around on the bottom with only their head and front legs protruding from their cells when feeding.

The adults are pretty moth-like flies. Young dragon-flies, May-flies, and, in fact, any small or medium-sized water insect, may be kept in the aquarium, but a netting or gauze cover should be placed over it or the insects may take wing and fly away at night.

For plants you may use watercress, duckweed, and, in fact, any sort of water-plant that you find growing in ponds, lakes, or brooks, with the exception of the slimy, soft growth, commonly called "frog-spittle" which should always be avoided.

If you have a fairly large aquarium you can add a lot to its beauty and to the health and happiness of its inmates by placing some growing potted water plants in it.

Pickerel-weed, arrowhead, sweet-flag, and pond-lilies may be planted in pots filled with peat and sand and lowered into the aquarium so that the leaves and flowers are above the surface.

Stones should then be piled around the pots on the bottom of the aquarium so as to hold the pots firmly in position and also to serve as a hiding-place for various forms of animal life. Always have your aquarium filled with water and the plants in position before collecting the animals and insects for it.

Never place the grotesque lava castles sold by dealers in an aquarium; because there are not useful. A few rough stones are far better and more satisfactory. When the aquarium is all prepared and the plants in place you may want to start shopping for the animals to live in it.

Freshwater Aquariums Manual

Chapter 1

Collecting The Specimens

The goldfish may, of course, be purchased from the nearest supplier, and small turtles, newts, and a few other creatures may at times be obtained from the same source.

The majority of your aquatic creatures must, however, be sought in their native haunts—in brooks, ponds, and lakes; and more than half the fun in having an aquarium consists in going out in the country and catching specimens to live in it.

The best place in which to collect is an old millpond or a small lake. Before starting out, however, you must have certain tools and gears for the work. These consist of a dip-net, a scoop, and several wide-mouthed glass jars which may be carried in a pail or basket.

The dip-net should be about 15 inches deep, and may be constructed from an old fish-net sewed onto a stout metal ring on a wooden handle at least 6 feet in length.

The scoop is the most important and essential implement. It consists of an old saucepan with the bottom punched full of holes, one side flattened out as shown in the cut, and a long wooden handle fastened firmly to it.

The dip-net is useful in capturing fish, turtles, frogs, and other lively creatures; but with the scoop you can dig and scrape up the sand and mud at the bottom of the pond, and in this way you will catch a lot which would otherwise escape from you.

Snails, insects, crustaceans, small fish, tadpoles, frogs, and turtles may all be caught in the scoop, and it is by far the most useful device you can find for pond collecting.

A small iron rake with a long handle is also very useful. With this you can rake aquatic weeds onto the shore, and by looking in this material you will find many live creatures.

The rake will also enable you to get fresh-water clams or mussels. As soon as your animals are caught, place them in jars of fresh, clean water, and keep them covered or protected from direct sunshine.

Water-plants may also be placed in the jars, and if a few plants are put in each jar they will prevent the captives from being shaken about and frightened or injured.

Chapter 2

The Best Season For

Collecting Water Animals

The best season for collecting is early in the spring. At this time a lot of aquatic creatures are breeding and are far easier to catch than they will be later in the summer, while many other species are sluggish and burrow in the mud until warm weather sets in.

You will be surprised at the variety of animal life that you will find in a small mill-pond and you will have no difficulty in collecting enough specimens to fill half a dozen aquariums. If you are interested in raising this class of animals I advise you to have several aquariums and to keep certain forms of animal life in each.

One may contain turtles and frogs with snails and plants; another herbivorous fish with newts or salamanders, tadpoles, water insects, snails, and plants; and a third may be devoted to carnivorous fish, such as bass, pickerel, eels, etc., with snails and plants.

Some people would not consider these aquatic creatures worthy of the name of pets, but I disagree. Many of our turtles, fishes, newts, and even frogs are capable of being tamed and will feed from the hand or will learn to recognize people at sight.

I have known kids who lived in country areas who have tamed wild fish in ponds and lakes merely by feeding them regularly, so that the trout, bass, perch, etc., would swim to their feeding spot when the kids approached and would take food from their fingers and even allow the youngsters to stroke them gently.

I have repeatedly kept water-salamanders that were so tame as to crawl up on one's finger if it was held out to them and, moreover, these newts would recognize a person at some distance and would show every sign of pleasure at one's approach.

Turtles, although possessing but little intelligence, will learn to recognize their master and will allow him to scratch or stroke their heads and will take food from his hand although they may be thrown into a perfect frenzy of fear at the approach of anyone else.

Many frogs will learn to eat from the hand and will be very tame in the presence of their owners, and I have even known water insects to become as thoroughly accustomed to human beings as to feed from one's fingers. In fact, about the only aquatic animal that cannot be considered as a pet is the snail. I have never yet seen a trained snail or a tame fresh-water clam.

Freshwater Aquariums Manual

Chapter 3

Water Animals Care And Feeding

Many water animals and plants will thrive in very dirty, foul water, but a dirty aquarium is an eyesore. Keep your aquarium clear as crystal, have the water fresh and pure at all times, and never feed more food than your pets will eat.

Where you have running water in the house, either from the city water-supply or from a tank or well, you may easily arrange your aquarium so that the water may be changed without disturbing the inmates.

This is by far the best method, for even if your aquarium is arranged with plant and animal life so balanced that the water is kept fresh, yet more or less sediment will accumulate and the water will become foggy or semi-opaque unless renewed with fresh water occasionally.

Freshwater Aquariums Manual

Chapter 4

Setting Up the Aquarium to Be Emptied and Filled Automatically

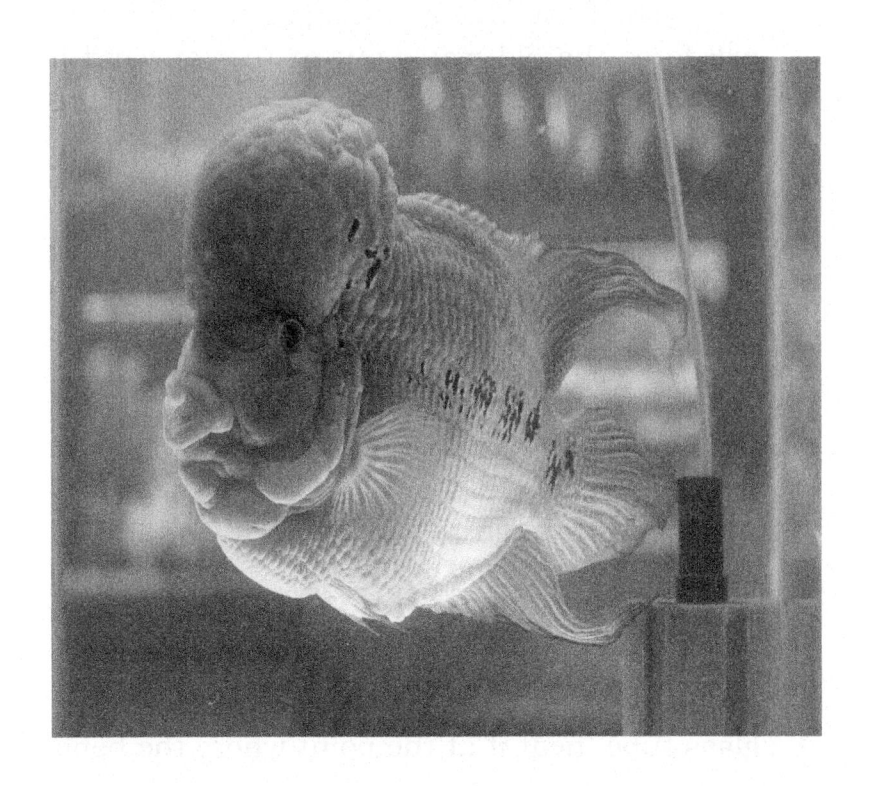

To arrange an aquarium so it may be emptied and filled automatically you should equip it with an overflow pipe opening into it at the height at which you wish to maintain the water.

This should be covered with fine wire or cloth gauze, and to replenish the water all you need to do is to insert a rubber tube from the nearest faucet down to within an inch or two of the bottom of the aquarium and turn on the water so it flows gently.

The fresh water coming in at the bottom will force the old water out at the top, and if the water is allowed to run for some time the aquarium will be completely filled with fresh, clean water.

When the aquarium has a metal or wooden bottom the overflow pipe is easily arranged; but if it is an all glass aquarium you must arrange a siphon to draw the water off. To do this, bend a piece of glass or metal tube—the glass is the better, as you can see the water through it—and bend it around at an angle.

If you use a metal tube, fill it with damp sand and plug the ends before bending; if a glass tube, heat it at the point where the bend is to be made in the flame of a Bunsen burner or gas-stove until it is bright red; it will then bend easily.

After the bent tube is prepared fill it with water, hold the two ends closed with your fingers, and without allowing the water to escape place the tube over one edge of the aquarium, with one end of the tube in the water and the other over a tub or other receptacle. Then remove your fingers from the ends of the tube, and if done properly a steady stream of water will flow from the aquarium through the siphon.

If water fails to flow you may want to start over again, but it is quicker and easier to suck on the end of the siphon until the water is drawn up into the tube.

If care is used there is no necessity of getting any water into your mouth, and if the tube is of glass you can always avoid this by watching the water as you suck and taking your mouth away as soon as the water begins to rise over the edge of the aquarium in the tube.

If a hose or tube is slipped over the outer end of the siphon the old water may be led directly into a sink or outside of the house. When using a siphon be sure to place fine gauze over the inner end or some of your animals may be drawn up through it.

As soon as the siphon commences to flow you may turn on the supply of fresh water, leading it to the bottom of the aquarium as already described.

If, while changing the water in this way, you scrub the glass inside with a long-handled brush, the vegetable growth on the glass may be easily removed and the dirt will be carried off in the overflow. This is a rather important matter, for vegetable growths on the glass give the aquarium a neglected, dirty appearance.

Chapter 5

Freshwater Snails

Fresh-water snails will eat this growth, but it will require several snails to keep it under control and, moreover, the snails themselves leave tracks on the glass.

Most water contains various chemical and mineral compounds in solution and, after standing awhile in an aquarium, these are deposited on the glass in the form of brownish, yellowish, or whitish films that must be scrubbed off as directed.

It is a mistake to remove all the inmates of an aquarium and scrub out the glass and then replace them. After an aquarium is once established, the animals and plants should be left undisturbed as much as possible.

Emptying the contents and scrubbing the glass is a method which may be followed with goldfish globes containing a few live creatures, but it is not a suitable method to follow in the case of a real aquarium.

Chapter 6

Cleaning The Aquarium

Never use soap, washing-powder, or other compounds in an aquarium; they are all injurious or fatal to the aquatic life. Aside from renewing the water from time to time and scrubbing off any mineral or vegetable deposits, on the glass, aquariums require very little care.

If any animal appears to be sick or dies, it should be removed at once by means of a long-handled net, and any food that remains after the inmates have been fed should also be removed. Decaying animal or vegetable matter soon renders the water, and it smells unpleasantly.

The inmates of an aquarium should be fed regularly and at stated times, and the proper food should be given according to the various forms of animal life.

The chances are that some of your aquarium pets will be carnivorous and others herbivorous and you will be compelled to feed both animal and vegetable substances to satisfy them all.

Ordinary goldfish food is very good for many fish; for turtles, for newts or salamanders, and for many other forms of aquatic life; but some species will not touch this, and other kinds of vegetable food must be fed.

Bread-crumbs, grated carrot, bits of lettuce leaves, finely cut or grated apple, and soaked rice may be given, and if you see any creature eat any of the substances you put in the aquarium, make a note of it and feed it regularly; you can always trust an aquatic animal to know what is best adapted to its digestive apparatus.

For the carnivorous animals—fish and insects—you can feed finely chopped lean beef or liver, earthworms cut into one-inch lengths, flies, crickets, other insects, and hard-boiled eggs.

Some aquatic creatures will eat one thing and some another, and some will decline all of those mentioned and must be tempted with bits of raw fish or fresh-water clams cut into small pieces.

Aim to determine just what your pets do and do not eat, and in a short time you will be able to furnish a bill of fare that will be suited to all the denizens of the aquarium.

Turtle

Freshwater Aquariums Manual

Aquarium Plant

Aquarium Snail

Moray Eel

Coral Eel

Freshwater Aquariums Manual

Eel

Sea Horse

Freshwater Aquariums Manual

Butterfly Cichlid

Discus Cichlid

Freshwater Aquariums Manual

Discus Fish

CPSIA information can be obtained
at www.ICGtesting.com
Printed in the USA
LVOW04s0255031215
465162LV00015B/179/P